The
Mouse Bride
A Chinese Folktale

Retold by Monica Chang
Illustrated by Lesley Liu

NORTHLAND PUBLISHING

Long ago,
there was a mouse village
in the corner of a farm wall.

In this village was a mouse farmer who had a
pretty daughter. Many of the young mice wanted
to marry her, but the farmer couldn't decide which
of them would be the best husband for her. He
thought and thought and finally decided on a test
that would show which of the young mice should
marry his daughter.

He built a platform on the top of the wall. His
daughter would climb to the platform and toss out
the wedding ribbon-ball. The one who caught it
would become her husband.

The young men gathered, ready to catch the ball
when the mouse maiden tossed it. Suddenly, they
all heard a *meow-meow* and the shadow of a big
black farm cat loomed across the crowd.

The cat pounced on and destroyed the platform
with one powerful bite. The mouse maiden fell
and was caught by a small mouse named
Aah-Lang, who led her to safety.

The cat made a mess of the village. Later that night, the farmer dreamed that the cat had caught his daughter. In his dream, he heard his daughter's screams and woke up, terrified.

He trembled and cried, then wrapped his blanket around himself and began to think. Finally, he said to himself, "It is too awful to worry about. I shall find my daughter a husband who is stronger than a cat. . . the strongest in the entire world."

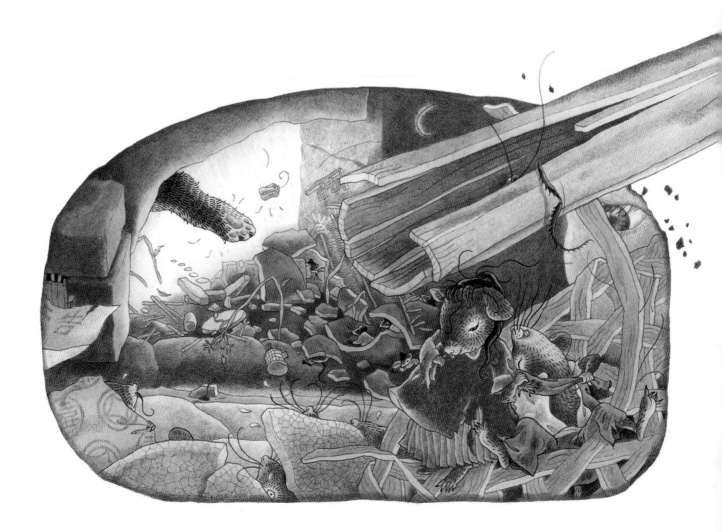

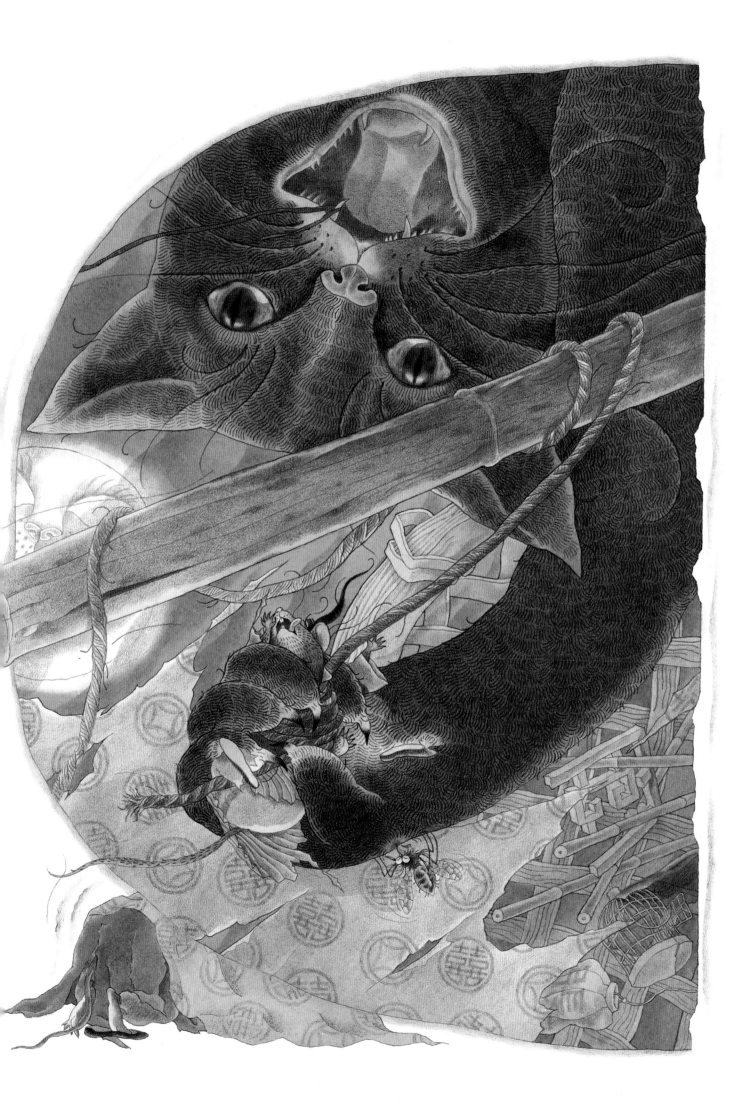

He thought and thought about who would be stronger than a cat. Soon a new day dawned and the light shone through a crack in the farmer's roof and fell on his face.

The farmer jumped up and cried, "I know! The Sun is the strongest in the world. There would be no light without the Sun, and nothing would grow. I want my daughter to marry the Sun."

With this, the farmer prepared himself for a journey and set out to look for the Sun.

Aah-Lang saw the farmer leave and, curious about where he might be going, decided to follow him.

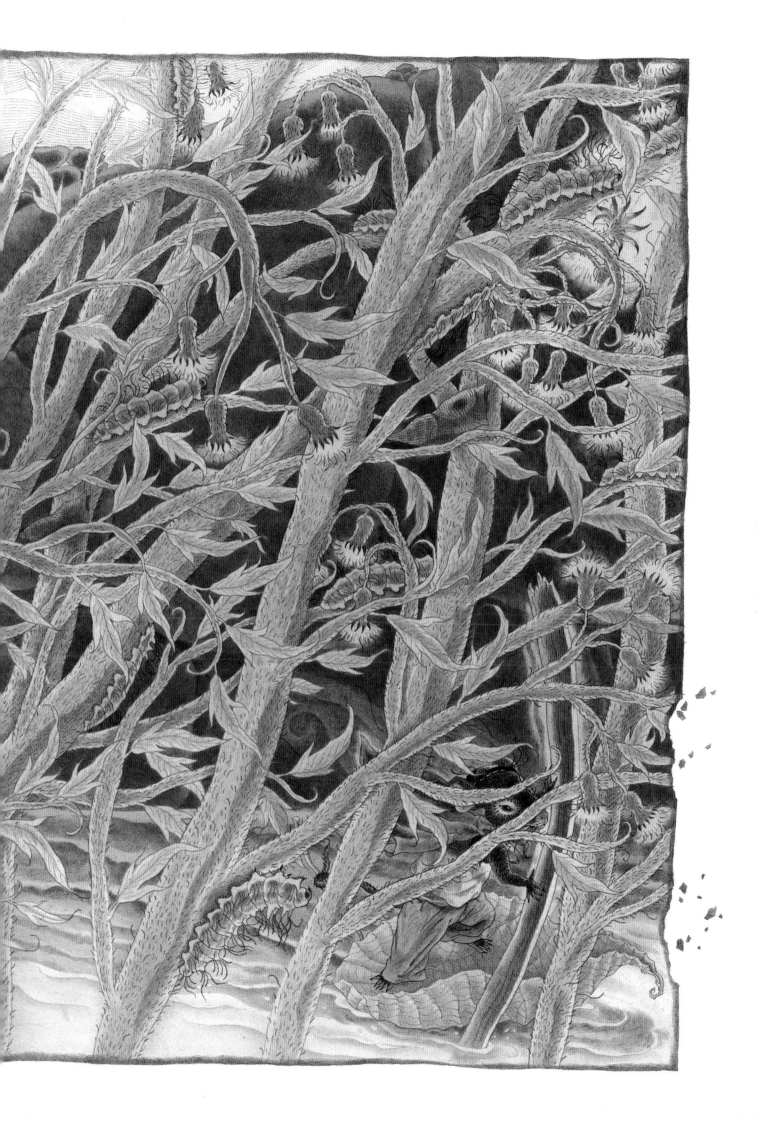

The farmer walked for a long time. Finally, he came to a mountain and climbed to the top. Facing the Sun, he asked, "Are you the strongest in the whole world?"

Radiating heat and light, the Sun proudly answered, "Of course I am the strongest in the whole world. Who else could create such heat and light?"

The farmer wiped the sweat from his brow and announced, "I am the mouse farmer and I want my daughter to marry you. . ."

Before he could complete his sentence, a Cloud came and covered the Sun.

The farmer called out again very loudly. "I am the mouse farmer and I want to marry my daughter to the strongest in the world. Are you the strongest, Cloud?"

The Cloud smiled and said, "Yes, I am the strongest. I am the only one who can stop the hot sunshine."

Before the Cloud could finish, a wind arose and blew the Cloud away, scattering it across the sky.

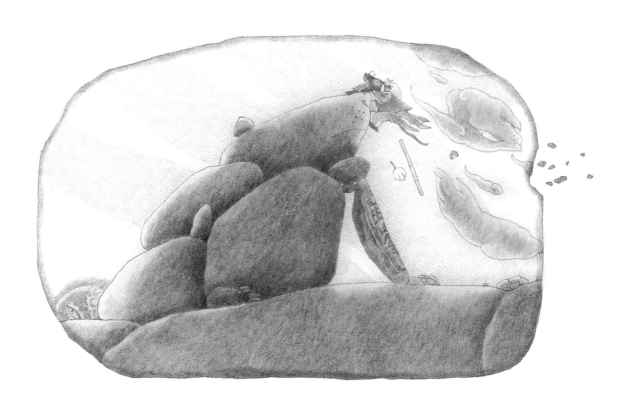

The farmer then asked the Wind the same question he'd asked of the Sun and the Cloud.

"Who can be stronger than me? I can blow away the Cloud as easily as I can blow the hat off your head. I can even blow you back to your home."

With that, the Wind blew a big gust that tossed the farmer into the sky. Aah-Lang, watching from a small distance, was blown into the nearby stream and floated down on the current.

The Wind continued to blow, and the farmer quickly found himself colliding with the village Wall. He fell to the ground and sat there, very dizzy.

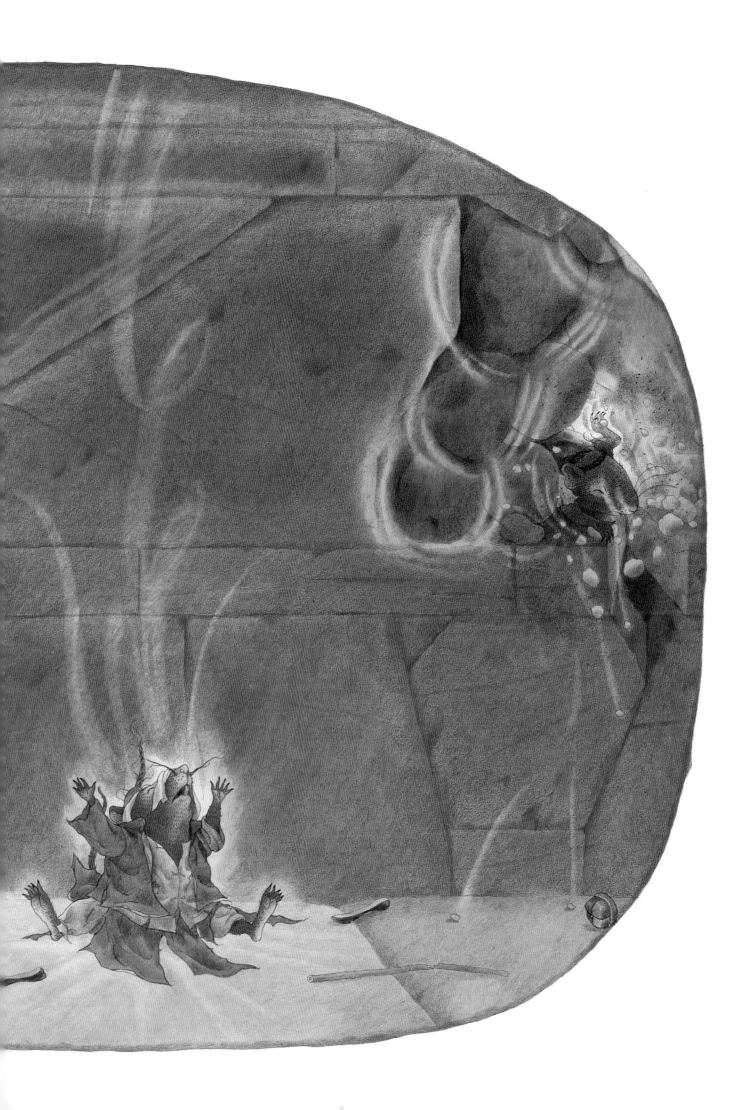

Then he looked up and said, "Wall, Wall, are you the strongest in the world? I want my daughter to be your bride."

The Wall replied, "I am not afraid of heaven or earth. I am the strongest in the world."

Suddenly, the farmer heard the Wall complain, "Ow, ow, ow!" Then he noticed a hole in the Wall and saw the small mouse Aah-Lang emerge through it. Aah-Lang picked up the farmer's hat and handed it to him.

Then the Wall said in a quiet voice, "I am not afraid of the Sun or the Cloud or the Wind. But I am afraid of the mouse who can make a hole in me with his sharp teeth."

Then the mouse farmer understood. Even though Aah-Lang was small, he had the skills to defeat the mightiest of foes. He said to Aah-Lang, "You are the strongest of all. I have decided that my daughter will marry you."

So on January third, the farmer's beautiful daughter was
brought on the carrying chair to be married to Aah-Lang.

Large and small mice helped carry the mouse bride
to the wedding. They also helped move her belongings.

After the wedding,
bride and bridegroom
saluted the parents:
Once, twice, three times
they bowed in respect.

Then they retired to their new house, and the guests feasted and played games and celebrated the marriage far into the night.

In honor of the mouse bride's wedding party, everyone in China goes to bed early on the night of January third.

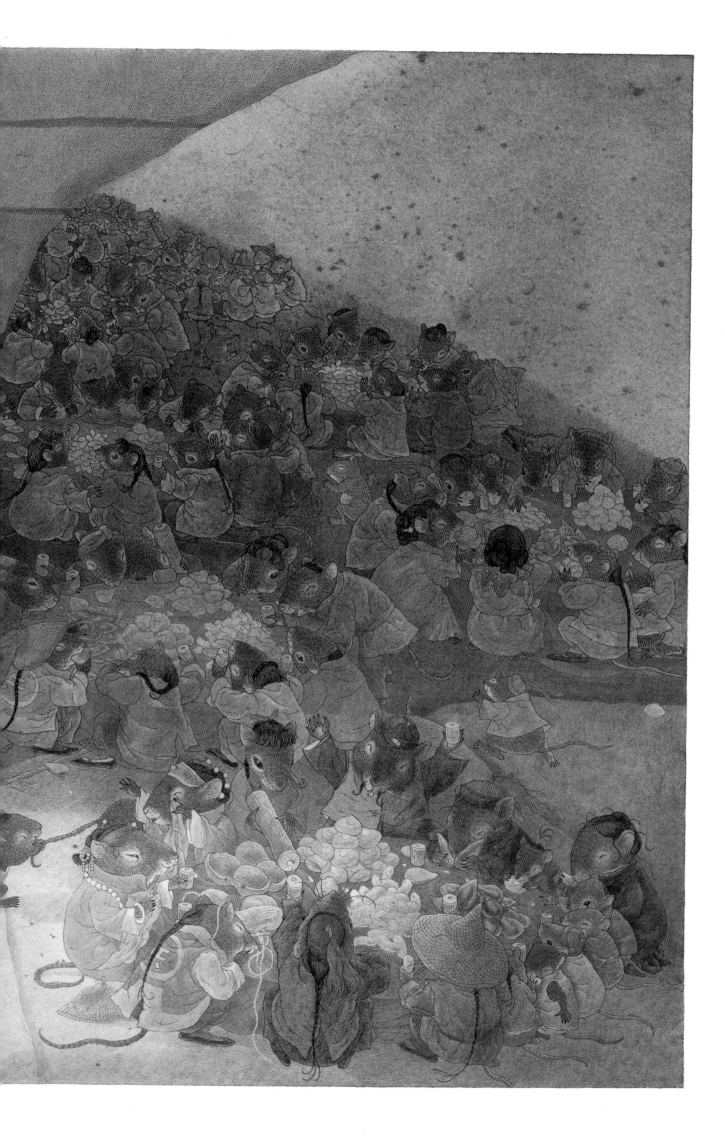

About the Creators

Ever since she was a little girl, Monica Chang has loved listening to all sorts of stories. Born in Taipei, Taiwan, in 1954, Ms. Chang graduated from Soochow University (Taiwan) and continued her studies at Skuba University in Japan, where she concentrated in folklore studies and children's literature. She presently works as an editor in the children's literature field.

Her published works include *The Women Island* and *The Pi Seller*, both belonging to the Chinese Folktale Series published by Yuan-Liou Publishing Company.

Beginning with a desire to create quality books for her son, Lesley Liu has been illustrating children's books for seven years. Born in Taipei, Taiwan, in 1960, Ms. Liu graduated from Fu-Shin Art School (Taiwan), and has worked as a designer in an advertising agency and as an illustrator in a publishing company.

Her published works include *The Bird of God*, winner of the 1990 Golden Dragon Award (Republic of China) and *Folk Art of Lu-Kong*, which won the Golden Dragon Award in 1991.

FIRST AMERICAN EDITION
ISBN 0-87358-533-X
Library of Congress Catalog Card Number 91-44296

Cataloging in Publication Data
Chang, Monica.
    The mouse bride : a Chinese folktale / retold by Monica Chang ; illustrated by Lesley Liu.
        32 p.
    Summary: A mouse goes to the sun, cloud, wind, and wall in search of the strongest husband for his daughter, only to find him among his own kind.
        ISBN 0-87358-533-X : 14.95
        [1. Folklore--China.] I. Liu, Lesley, ill. II. Title.
    PZ8.1 .C359Mo 1992   91-44296
    398.24'5293233--dc20   CIP

Manufactured in Taiwan

5-92/5M/0394